Human Traits & Follies

Previous Books:

Exposed to Winds
[Selected poems]

Construction Delay Claims
[Performance measurements]

Anecdotes of Would-be Experts
[Business experiences]

Thoughts in a Maze
[Various mysteries]

Trials and Errors
[Life experiences]

Characters
[A tribute to past friends]

Oddities
[False assumptions]

Connections
[Human beliefs & behaviors]

Conclusions Volumes I & II
[Reaching conclusions – right or wrong]

My Best Dog Days
[Autobiographical sketches]

Investment Fundamentals
Including Their Effect on Pensions

Our Support Systems
[The prop ups in our lives]

About My Books
[A synopsis of each book]

Human Traits & Follies

by

Arthur O.R. Thormann

Specfab Industries Ltd.

Edmonton, Alberta

2015

Library and Archives Canada Cataloguing in Publication

Thormann, Arthur O. R. (Arthur Otto Rudolf), 1934-, author
    Human Traits & Follies / by Arthur O.R. Thormann.

ISBN 978-0-9916849-5-3 (pbk.)

    1. Human beings. 2. Virtue. 3. Vice. 4. Human behaviour.
I. Title. II. Title: Human traits and follies.

BD450.T56 2015   128'.3   C2015-900767-4

Publisher: Specfab Industries Ltd.
                        13559 - 123A Avenue
                        Edmonton, Alberta, Canada
                        T5L 2Z1
                        Telephone: 780-454-6396

Publication assistance by

PAGEMASTER
PUBLISHING
PageMaster.ca

Cover Designs: Front: Photo of a Chinese figurine
                        Back: Photo of an African figurine

Empires came, Empires went,
But the people carried on;
In tradition of lore,
They built us more,
To create a bloc
That makes
Us one.

♥

"A toast to the People!"

I dedicate this book to my cousin Bernie Jeske

My gratitude goes to my daughter Nancy,
and to my friend Pam Sigvaldason,
for their valued advice.
All mistakes remaining are entirely mine.

Preface

This book explores how human beings may have been created, how they united themselves, built and lost empires, reached the present stage of development, and now head towards possible destruction.

The Chinese people are probably the earliest group of human beings who have successfully united and who have stayed successfully united. Furthermore, the Chinese people successfully assimilated with other groups of people. The Americans of the U.S.A. reached a similar success, of course.

However, Europeans have a dismal record. It is interesting how early Europeans, many hundreds of years back, split themselves apart, and are now trying to reunite themselves, despite their differences and mutual hates that separated and still separate them. The Europeans could do much better if they set aside their warring history and united themselves to their mutual advantage.

Particularly, the book explores some human traits that either support or hinder human development.

Human beings are able to use their traits remarkably better than other animals. Take the way humans reason; the way they consciously create; the way they send themselves messages; the way they plan their future; to list a few; also, how these traits affected history, and how they affect contemporary actions. It is wise to remember that all actions, even inactions, send messages – often unintended messages. Therefore, all actions must be carefully considered.

The ability to appraise human traits is especially important in our time. In the final analysis, human traits, and actions caused by human traits, will always form the basis of either beneficial or destructive consequences.

The titles of the chapters, like *Empire Builders*, *Aspiration to be President*, *Follow the Leader*, and *Majority & World Control*, give some indication of the traits that are being explored. Take majority rule: though favored by democracies, it must be questioned, because it also led to the execution of Socrates in Athens, and the election of the Nazi Party in Germany.

Hopefully, the study of these human traits, and various topics, will lead us to some useful insights.

I chose a sleeping Chinaman for the front cover. Don't you love the old fellow? I certainly do. He's been sleeping for a long time, and when he awakes, we will all know it. The back cover depicts a possible ancestor of the human race. Treat him kindly.

Arthur O.R. Thormann

February 2015

Contents

Introduction

Life is full of puzzling questions, many unanswerable, and to reach a conclusion on unanswerable questions is, at best, a speculation. Nevertheless, such speculations keep the mind active, and, thus, serve a useful purpose.

A puzzling question is how our various races of human beings developed, and one speculation is that we all originated in Africa, and we all came from one set of parents. Scientists do not have a big problem with this speculation, but I do. Take cats, for example. Cats vary from lions to tigers to panthers to pussy cats. How would all these variations have originated from one set of parents? But human beings having a single set of original parents poses another question, namely, how did its own creation or duality principle[*] take place? This question should stymie all those who reject the Bible's explanation.

The various conflicts between human beings pose more questions. With the development of these conflicts, mostly wars, a hatred between the various

---

[*] By "duality principle" in this case, I mean the necessity of a male and a female to create an offspring.

nations also developed, especially in Europe, although the Americans took part in the conflicts in Europe during the twentieth century. But through their involvement in the European conflicts, the Americans developed into the most powerful nation in the world – not because of their size but because of their advanced technology, and their buildup of armory. The Russians tried to match the Americans, but fell short. Then, terrorists sprang up to fight the Europeans and the Americans, and terrorists' hatred is hard to explain, which poses the question how to deal with them, other than to declare war on them and kill them.

Human beings built empires and lost empires, and this poses more questions. However, when one studies the Chinese dynasties, one can only admire them. The Chinese are the earliest civilization that still exists today. They went through wars waged upon them and survived. They even managed to assimilate with their enemies. In the latter part of the twentieth century, they began developing into a world power. They have the manpower; they have the atomic bomb; and they have the financial clout. We would be well advised to maintain their friendship. In my experience, the Chinese are also less rude than the Europeans.

Some of the answers have to do with the way human beings treat each other. Unfriendliness and rudeness are rampant, for example. Bill Bryson tells us in his book *Neither Here Nor There* of some of the unfriendly encounters he has had during his travels in Europe. I have had a few similar experiences in Europe, which seem to be lacking in North America.

When I paid a visit to Germany after twenty-one years of absence, I had a few encounters with rudeness that puzzled me. One time, I stood at a street corner in Frankfurt, waiting for the traffic light to change, when a middle-aged man shoved me roughly aside. I gave him a surprised look, expecting an apology, but he just glowered at me, as if to let me know that I had deprived him of his usual spot. A word to do with the rear end came to my mind, but I quickly ignored it. A few similar experiences on this trip made me glad to return to a more polite and tolerant Canada.

I offer a few more truly puzzling situations to my readers, some involving human strengths but mostly human weaknesses, such as the obsession with greed and envy, our blind obeisance to questionable leaders, the fascinations with fatalism and eternal life, the prospect of world control, the enemy within us, the danger of fatigue leading to burnout, obvious human and godly design flaws, as well as the impossibility of "Peace on Earth."

Nevertheless, any conclusions we could possibly reach regarding these puzzling situations only lead to more puzzling questions, and puzzling questions that are devoid of acceptable conclusions seem to be never-ending in our lives.

Creation & Progress of Human Beings

Most of us are familiar with the Biblical account of the creation of human beings, but the Sumerian account is just as interesting. Sumer was the land of "civilized kings" and flourished in Mesopotamia, now modern Iraq. The Sumerians were the earliest non-Semitic civilized people. Their religion comprised of hundreds of gods – each Sumerian city was guarded by its own god – and they were the servants of their gods.

The Sumerian creation myth can be found on a tablet in Nippur, an ancient city founded circa 5000 BC. It claims that in the beginning the gods ruled the Earth, and when they first came to Earth, there was much work to be done. These gods toiled heavily and began to mutiny against their labor. Anu, the god of the gods, agreed that their labor was too great, and his son Enki proposed to create man to bear the labor; he did so with the help of his half-sister Ninki. To do so, they killed a god and mixed his body and blood with clay to create the first human being in their likeness. This first man was created in Eden, a Sumerian word meaning "flat terrain."

(Since the Sumerian creation myth goes back

before the Biblical creation account was written, it is quite possible that the Biblical creation-account authors got much of their material from the Sumerians. You may recall that the Biblical account also talks about creating man in "our" likeness – note the plural!)

Erich von Däniken would have a field day with this myth, I think, since it supports his theory that aliens first came to Earth, and that human beings were created by these aliens. Both the Sumerian and the Biblical accounts of creation certainly support such a theory – substitute "aliens" for "gods" and these accounts start making sense. Nevertheless, science has its problems with this theory.

It makes more sense to science that human beings were created from the same mire as other beings on Earth, and this might well be correct. If so, it also makes sense that this "mire" was located in Africa, and, that after a certain gestation and development period, human beings started to migrate out of Africa – first to Europe and the Middle East, and then to other parts of Earth. After spending many years in colder climates, the skin of these migrant human beings eventually turned lighter, and other climate influences also changed a few more of their physical features. The Earth's climates can certainly transform physical features of human beings. We can observe some similar transformations in the animal world: for example, the white furs of polar bears in the Arctic region, and the furs of rabbits turning white in winter.

From the Middle East, the migrants moved further east to India and Mongolia, and from there to Korea and China, and from Korea they crossed the Korea Strait to Japan. They also moved further north, to Siberia and eventually crossed the Bering Strait to Alaska, before migrating further south again, to other parts of the Americas. Alternatively, a continental drift could have separated America from Africa and taken with it the so-called American Indians – originally Africans. This entire scenario would explain the theory of Africa being the home country of all human beings.

Another alternative scenario, although equally plausible, would be that the racial differences of human beings and human beings themselves may have originated separately in various parts of Earth, just as different trees sprang up in various parts of Earth.

Mind you, regardless of which creation theory you accept, all of this must have happened hundreds of thousands of years ago, even millions of years ago, which poses another question: Why did it take human beings such an enormous amount of time to make the progress that seemed to have happened only less than ten thousand years ago? This does not make much sense, unless the human progress was suddenly aided by aliens, which both the Sumerian and the Biblical accounts seem to support. Furthermore, the help of aliens could also account for humans building the pyramids, for the development of their written language, and for a host of other so-called miracles on Earth.

Empire Builders

Human beings have been empire builders for thousands of years. The reason for this aspiration is speculative, at best. It could be the desire of leaders to increase their following; it could be a desire to increase their tax base; it could be the irresistible drive to increase their territory; or it could be plain and simple envy between leaders to become the greatest and most powerful on Earth. In any case, all these empires were relatively short-lived. The last of the modern empires, namely the British Empire, finally came to an end when its last remaining colony, Hong Kong, was turned over to the People's Republic of China on July 1st 1997.

The Wikipedia lists 213 of the largest empires in world history, some of them going back three and four thousand years, the biggest of them with more than twenty percent of the world's population at the time of their existence. No doubt, smaller empires existed even before recorded history to satisfy human leaders' desires. These desires may not always be megalo-maniac. The Aztecs, for example, needed many human bodies to offer their gods; the larger their empire, the larger the number of available humans that they could sacrifice, and the Incas built their empire mainly for scientific reasons. Both the Aztecs and the Incas lost their empires because the invading Conquistadors simply destroyed them. The reason for this destruction is unclear, unless the Conquistadors felt threatened by the Aztecs and Incas. The American Indians were certainly a threatening people, as the Vikings found out when they tried to settle on the eastern coast of North America in the tenth and eleventh centuries.

However, most empire builders strived for territorial gain. Territorial gain would assure them an increase in natural resources, in addition to an increase in taxpayers. The British Empire was one of the largest territorial empires, consisting of 33.7 million km^2 – circa 20% of the world's population in 1938. The Mongol Empire came next in size, with 33 million km^2 and ≈ 25% of the world's population in the 13th century. The Russian Empire was next in size, with 22.8 million km^2 but only ≈ 10% of the world's population in 1913. The Spanish Empire consisted of 19.4 million km^2 and comprised ≈ 12% of the world's population in the 17th century. Although population gain came with territorial gain, territorial gain seemed more important. Territorial gain was also Napoleon's and Hitler's strife. Neither of these leaders was interested in population gain when they invaded

Russia. Hitler even made it quite clear that he was only trying to gain more *Lebensraum* (room to live). Empire builders' strife for *Lebensraum* may even extend to space in the future. However, none of the past empire builders had purely altruistic intents, unless one calls sacrifices to their gods altruistic, which is questionable.

It is evident that empire building depends mainly on territorial gain. Take Russia, today. With over 17 million km^2 Russia is the largest country in the world, but has, relative to its size, a fairly small population of 142 million people (just over eight people per km^2). Yet, Russia is one of the most powerful states. Its mineral and energy resources are the largest in the world, making Russia one of the largest producers of oil and natural gas globally. Russia is also one of the five recognized nuclear-weapons-states (NWS) and has probably the largest stockpile of weapons of mass destruction. Besides, Russia has had some significant technological achievements, such as the first human-made satellite and the first man in space. Nevertheless, Russia still seems to aim at enlarging its territory. For example, it welcomed the addition of Ukrainian's Crimea recently; now it seems poised to encourage Ukrainian rebels to secede a part of the Ukraine, hopefully to join Russia. This has led Western Powers to impose sanctions on Russia, which could lead to another Cold War, Mikhail Gorbachev has warned as recently as November 8th 2014. He said the West has "succumbed to triumphalism" after the collapse of the USSR in 1991. In addition, Russia's President Vladimir Putin has warned the West that their sanctions would not only harm Russia but also the rest of the world. Considering Russia's economic strength, President Putin may well be correct. He has discussed the issue with German Chancellor Angela Merkel in a sideline meeting of the G-20 Summit of November 2014. Angela Merkel is trying to maintain friendly relations with Vladimir Putin, of course, but even she is unwilling to see the Ukraine broken up.

The state title "empire" has disappeared with emperors, of course, but in effect we still have empires; our most powerful modern states (empires) are the USA, Russia, and China. Russia is presently (November 2014) out of favor, because of its alleged involvement with the Ukrainian rebels. When Russia's President Vladimir Putin approached Canada's Prime Minister Stephen Harper in a friendly manner to shake his hand at the G20 Summit in November 2014, Harper told him, "Well, I guess I'll shake your hand, but I have only one thing to say to you: you need to get out of Ukraine." Putin just turned around and muttered, "That's impossible, because we're not there." Mr. Harper felt good about having given the powerful Russian a piece of his mind, and Mr. Putin probably thought, "What a foolish man." British Prime Minister David Cameron also criticized the Russian leader for his actions regarding the Ukraine. However, Mr. Putin delivered a few of his own warnings.

Besides criticizing the West's sanctions, he told France there would be serious consequences if France fails to deliver a war ship delayed by Ukrainian events, and he told Germany that 300,000 German jobs could be at risk by refusing contracts with Russia.

In an interview with German television broadcast on November 16th 2014, Mr. Putin voiced his concern with far-right national elements in Ukraine and against what Moscow perceives as the repression of Russian-speakers in the region: "I'll say this bluntly: we're very concerned that the desire could arise to use ethnic cleansing. We're afraid about a drift toward neo-Nazism in the region." In response to a question about whether Russia was arming the rebels, as contended by both Kyiv and the West, Mr. Putin said merely that "anyone waging a fight that they believe fair will find weapons." He stressed that without such arms the rebels would be quickly destroyed by the Ukrainian forces – something Russia "does not want, and will not allow." His comments went further in emphasizing Moscow's willingness to support the separatists than ever before. This is understandable because of the

Russian heritage of the separatists.

Although Mr. Putin did not outright admit that Russia is supplying arms to the Ukrainian rebels, his comments leave no doubt about that. Furthermore, his comments leave no doubt that the Ukrainian rebels' cause is fair, and that Moscow supports their cause, even if the West disagrees with Moscow. On the other hand, the West seems to have no difficulty supporting the Syrian rebels fighting their government because they think the rebels' cause is fair. Regarding both factions of rebels, the only difference between the Ukraine and Syria is that the West supports the Ukraine and Russia supports Syria against their rebels.

Modern "empire" builders are still striving for territorial gains – even Russia, whose territory is already the largest in the world. Presently, there are over two hundred territorial disputes worldwide. Note, however, that the aspiration of modern "empire" builders is leaning more towards financial advantages than towards territorial gains, since sanctions applied against each other are financial in nature. Additionally, modern "empire" builders shy away from using their military forces against each other to gain their ends.

The exception may be a Sunni group of "empire" builders known as Islamic State (IS). The Islamic State group is presently (November 2014) active in

Iraq and Syria, and making inroads at Egypt and Libya. On June 29th 2014, the group proclaimed a worldwide caliphate, and its leader, Abu Bakr al-Baghdadi, was named its caliph. As caliphate, it claims religious authority over all Muslims, and aims to bring Muslim-inhabited regions of the world under its control.[*] If one can believe the predictions in George Friedman's book *The Next 100 Years* (see page 36), IS may eventually control the north half and eastern part of Africa, as well as the Middle East, and regions all the way into the Far East, the Philippines, and the northern regions north of India all the way to China. If successful, this group would control a vast region with a power to be reckoned with.

There is another exception: George Friedman also predicts a similar expansion, and power play, by Mexico, north into the United States of America. With millions of illegal immigrants from Mexico to the USA every year, it is very plausible that Mexican control in the US will eventually become manifest, although very much unwanted by the US. In addition, Mexico may eventually aspire to regain her territory lost after the 1846-1848 war with the USA. Hence, territorial "empire" building is by no means a thing of the past!

One example is the Crimean peninsula of the

---

[*]See the Wikipedia for details

Ukraine. Following the Russian Revolution in 1917, Crimea became a republic of the USSR. Then, in 1954, Crimea was transferred to the Ukrainian Soviet Socialist Republic, and in 1991, it became the Autonomous Republic of Crimea within the newly independent Ukraine. Then, in 2014, Crimea became the subject of a territorial dispute between the Ukraine and Russia, and Russia signed a treaty of accession with the then self-declared independent Republic of Crimea, absorbing it into the Russian Federation.

Thus, even a state like Russia that consists already of the largest territory on Earth will not hesitate to expand its region.

Majority & World Control

People who democratically elect a group of representatives to act on their behalf are under the mistaken
belief that this elected group of representatives arrives
at its decisions collectively. However, the task of
arriving at decisions is usually left to a smaller, elite
faction within the group. Every group has an elite
faction, unless the group is too small to have such a
separate faction. Members of the elite faction are
smart, dress smart, and act smart. They consider the
actions that should be taken by the main group and
come up with their final recommendations. Members
of the elite faction do not mind opposing views to
suggestions among themselves, but when they reach a
consensus, they abhor further opposition, especially
from the main group. The consensus of the elite
faction is then submitted to the main group for action,
and the main group is expected to agree with the elite
faction's recommendations. In other words, majority
rule becomes majority control, especially when
groupthink of an elite faction is involved. This is how
most democratic groups operate all over the world.

Nevertheless, it is one of the basic concepts of

democracies to depend on majority rule, and majority rule gets it wrong sometimes, even with an elite faction's control and recommendation. Examples of getting it wrong are when an Athens majority convicted Socrates to death, and when a German majority elected the Nazi Party. Wrong decisions by majorities occur often enough in the world that some thought should be given to making timely corrections.

In smaller groups, a minority could appeal to a recognized neutral party, like a retired judge, or an arbitrator, to render an opinion, or a decision that could change the outcome of the majority rule, providing that the bylaws or rules of the group accept a judge's opinion or an arbitrator's decision. Such a provision works for small groups but is impracticable for an entire nation. When an entire nation gets it wrong, it is almost impossible to achieve a timely correction. In fact, such a correction may even be impossible when a dictator takes over and creates new laws or rules that prevent such correction, for example his or her ouster. All democracies are aware of the dangers of majority-rule getting it wrong and try to invent ways for its correction, but correcting mistakes is always more difficult than making them.

Even the majority of the Supreme Court can get it wrong. A case in point is when Dred Scott, a former slave who had moved to the free state of Illinois and free territory of Wisconsin moved back to the slave state of Missouri and was again subjected to slavery. Scott appealed to the Supreme Court. The court ruled against Scott on the basis that all blacks, whether they were slaves or not, were not and could never become citizens; thus, the US Declaration of Independence, which clearly states that "all men are created equal," does not apply to them. Chief Justice Roger Taney argued that "it is too clear for dispute that the enslaved African race were not intended to be included, and formed no part of the people who framed and adopted this declaration." The American Civil War broke out four years later, in 1861.

Dangerous outcomes can also result from some people's support of "might is right." Take the OPEC meeting of November 27th 2014. The majority of OPEC's member states were in favor of cutting their oil production by 5%, but, with Saudi Arabia's opposition, they decided against it. In this case, Saudi Arabia was the "might" that resulted in the overruling of the majority. The majority of OPEC's member states could not afford to cut production without Saudi Arabia's support, and, therefore, had to side with Saudi Arabia, even though they felt this was wrong. Similarly, actions by the USA are accepted by other nations, not because the actions of the USA are right, but because of the USA's accepted "might."

I want to end this chapter with a few comments on world control, particularly financial world control, but also deistic world control. During the inflationary period of the 1970s, I was consumed with the notion that the financial world was controlled by a number of moguls, who, when the masses got too rich, would simply start another round of inflation to keep the wealth of the masses in check.[*] To protect their own wealth, the moguls would make sure that their investments kept up with inflation, such as prime real estate,[†] since the capital of bonds, for example, would be essentially destroyed by inflation. This capital destruction through inflation also affected the assets of pension funds, which were heavily invested in bonds at the time.

This notion of world control was not new, to be sure. There are, in fact, various organizations that

---

[*] Prior to the second half of the twentieth century, our moguls consisted largely of bankers, insurers, miners, and industrialists; then, during the second half of the twentieth century, they were joined by oil producers and technologists.

[†] During the second half of the twentieth century, oil-rich Arabian moguls bought up loads of real estate in Europe, America, and other parts of the world; then, towards the end of the twentieth century, moguls from Hong Kong joined the Arabian real-estate buyers and caused a skyrocketing of real estate, especially in the housing sector. This, in turn, caused ordinary people who wanted to buy houses or condos to commit themselves to unrealistic mortgages, eventually causing the world-wide financial crises in 2008, a crisis that had not been equaled since the 1920s, a crisis that even the moguls could not stop, and governments had to step in to bail out the moguls.

claim, or are alleged to have, links to the original Bavarian Illuminati[*] or similar secret societies. They are frequently alleged to scheme to control world affairs, i.e., masterminding events and planting agents in governments and large corporations to gain political power and establish a New World Order. However, World Control should not be confused with World Government, which is the notion of a single common political authority for all humanity. US past President Harry S. Truman envisioned the United Nations to eventually fulfill this role. He also envisioned a World Court to settle all human differences.

After a while, I dropped the notion of financial-world control by a number of moguls. In reality, the financial world is too complex to be controlled by a small number of moguls. It is, in fact, controlled by a set of financial rules, which cannot be manipulated in total. At best, one can try to understand these financial rules and try to roll with their punches, as it were.

A belief in mogul-control of the financial world

---

[*] The Bavarian Illuminati was a secret society founded May 1st 1776. Its goals were to oppose superstition, obscurantism, and religious influence over public life, as well as abuses of state power. The Illuminati, Free Masonry, and other secret societies were outlawed in the 1780s by the Bavarian ruler Charles Theodore with the encouragement of the Catholic Church. Following the 1780s, the Illuminati were vilified by conservative and religious critics, who claimed that they continued underground and were responsible for the French Revolution.

is akin to the belief in an emotional God, a God who causes benefaction or destruction at a whim, rather than a belief in a set of universal laws that represent the supreme existence, laws that impartially control everything in the Universe. The key word here is "impartially." One can pray for partiality, but one will not receive it. Nevertheless, these universal laws, just as financial rules, may work to one's benefit quite often, but this does not happen whimsically, or by design, it happens accidentally, or "impartially." One would do well to remember this.

Enerpolitical Considerations

Every person requires energy to sustain and move the body, and industry requires energy to create its products. When a country runs short of the supply of energy, its government gets involved. Hence: enerpolitical considerations.

Twelve countries have joined OPEC for enerpolitical considerations, mostly on the supply side. OPEC stands for Organization of the Petroleum Exporting Countries, an international group and economic cartel whose aim is to coordinate the policies of the oil-producing countries, i.e., secure a steady income to the member states. The member states consist of Iraq, Kuwait, Iran, Saudi Arabia, Venezuela, Libya, the United Arab Emirates, Qatar, Algeria, Nigeria, Ecuador, and Angola. Their headquarters are located in Vienna, Austria.

OPEC held a meeting on November 27th 2014 and, against the advice of the majority of its members, it decided to maintain its daily production target. This decision immediately caused a 10% drop of the oil-price per barrel in the markets. The main reason for OPEC's decision was the economic threat to its members of the US boom in fracking for shale oil, and the consequent US highest oil production in three decades.

What is interesting is that this *minority* wish to maintain the daily production ended up as OPEC's decision. Iran's Oil Minister Bijan Namdar Zanganeh pushed for a 1.5 million barrels-per-day reduction,[*] which amounts to 5% of OPEC's daily output, but he was up against Saudi Arabia's Oil Minister Ali Al-Naimi, who wanted to maintain the daily output. Mr. Zanganeh said, after the meeting, that lower oil prices are no guarantee of significant reduction in US shale-oil output. He said that Iran can boost its daily output by one million barrels within two months if international sanctions on the country's economy and oil industry are removed. The US and the European Union have imposed these sanctions on Iran because of Iran's nuclear program.

Mr. Al-Naimi, whose position obviously controlled the OPEC decision, said that "the spread of misleading information and speculation" had contributed to the 40% fall in the price of oil. Mr. Al-Naimi added that if producer countries outside OPEC want to restrict oil output they are welcome: "We are not going to cut – certainly Saudi Arabia is not going

---

[*] Non-OPEC oil producers were also willing to cut their daily production by 500,000 barrels.

to cut." (This last remark certainly makes it obvious who controlled OPEC's decision.) Mr. Al-Naimi said he was not happy about the falling oil price, but added: "Current prices do not encourage investment in any form of energy, but they stimulate global economy growth, leading ultimately to an increase in global demand and a slowdown in the growth of supplies." His is a very enerpolitical position, you must admit.

However, here is what Gail Tverberg[*] says about low oil prices:

> "In my view, a rapid drop in oil prices is likely a symptom that we are approaching a debt-related collapse... Underlying this debt-related collapse is the fact that we seem to be reaching the limits of a finite world. There is a growing mismatch between what workers in oil importing countries can afford, and the rising real costs of extraction, including associated governmental costs. This has been covered up to date by rising debt, but at some point, it will not be possible to keep increasing the debt sufficiently. The timing of collapse may not be immediate. Low oil prices take a while to work their way through the

---

[*] Gail Tverberg is the author of *Our Finite World*. She has an M.S. from the University of Illinois, Chicago.

system. It is also possible that the world's financiers will put off a major collapse for a while longer, through more QE [quantitative easing] or more programs related to QE. For example, actually getting money into the hands of customers would seem to be temporarily helpful."

OPEC supplies 40% of the world's oil use. At the present time (November 2014) the oil production in the world results in a two million barrel per day surplus, causing oil prices to slump to their lowest levels since 2009. OPEC's members can still produce oil at a profit despite these low oil prices, but it is doubtful that heavy-oil producers can maintain a profit for long, and that is probably what Saudi Arabia is counting on. Saudi Arabia sees the US's production at its highest level in thirty years, while OPEC's share shrank to its lowest level in that period. Thus, OPEC plays a large role in the world's political arena regarding energy policy, or, what I term enerpolitical considerations.

To deal with critical future energy shortages, most countries have established an energy policy. Such a policy usually deals with energy production, distribution, and consumption. In the United Kingdom, the current focus is on reforming the electricity market and improving the energy efficiency. In the

United States, however, no comprehensive, long-term energy policy has yet been forthcoming. The US energy policies are dominated by crisis-mentality thinking, promoting expensive quick fixes.

Nevertheless, due to new technologies, such as fracking, the US has in 2014 resumed its former role of top oil producer in the world. Russia's energy policy calls for an increase in energy efficiency, reducing impact on the environment, and sustainable development. Russia also signed a deal with China: in return for $25 billion in loans to Russian oil companies, Russia will supply China with crude oil via new pipelines for the next twenty years. China's main concern is ensuring adequate energy supply to sustain economic growth, even at the expense of being the world's largest emitter of greenhouse gases.

India's energy policy is defined by the country's mushrooming energy deficit. Its increased focus is on developing alternative sources of energy. 70% of India's electricity generation is achieved using fossil fuels and is hindered by domestic coal shortages. India also has ambitious plans to increase its nuclear power industries. The country has five nuclear reactors under construction and plans to construct eighteen more by 2025.

Ideally, though, a long-term energy policy should include phasing out the use of fossil fuels. Germany has an energy policy worth mentioning. The German economy ranks fourth in the world by GDP, sixth in global energy consumption, and is one of Europe's largest consumers of electricity. Germany's current key energy policy is an "energy turnaround," or "energy transformation." In other words, Germany intends to eliminate the use of nuclear power by 2022 – some plants have already been closed prior to their intended retirement dates. To replace nuclear power, Germany intends to temporarily continue, but phasing out, the use of fossil fuels, and concentrate more on wind power, solar power, biofuel production, and energy conservation. It is an ambitious policy, but worth pursuing, and other countries should take a closer look at it.

In the final analysis, energy consumption is a world-wide concern; it should be addressed on a world-wide scale, and it should achieve world-wide agreement. This is where enerpolitical considerations of individual countries can prove most useful.

Nuclear-Weapon Tease

In the 1960s, we were genuinely afraid of nuclear war; today, the threat of using nuclear weapons has become nothing more than a tease. Take the new Military Doctrine that Russian President Vladimir Putin has signed on Friday December 26th 2014. Here are some comments from the Associated Press that were published on the same day:

> Russia identified NATO as the nation's No. 1 military threat and raised the possibility of a broader use of precision conventional weapons to deter foreign aggression under a new military doctrine signed by President Vladimir Putin on Friday…The new doctrine, which comes amid tensions over Ukraine, reflected the Kremlin's readiness to take a stronger posture in response to what it sees as US-led efforts to isolate and weaken Russia…It says Russia could employ nuclear weapons in retaliation for the use of nuclear or other weapons of mass destruction against the country or its allies, and also in the case of aggression involving conventional

weapons that "threaten the very existence" of the Russian state…But for the first time, the new doctrine says Russia could use precision weapons "as part of strategic deterrent measures." The document does not spell out when and how Moscow could resort to such weapons. Examples of precision conventional weapons include ground-to-ground missiles, air- and submarine-launched cruise missiles, guided bombs and artillery shells…Among other things, the paper mentions the need to protect Russia's interests in the Arctic, where the global competition for its vast oil and other resources has been heating up as the Arctic ice melts…Russia has relied heavily on its nuclear deterrent and lagged behind the US and its NATO allies in the development of precision conventional weapons. However, it has recently sped up its military modernization, buying large numbers of new weapons and boosting military drills…The program envisages the deployment of new nuclear-tipped inter-continental ballistic missiles, the construction of nuclear submarines and a sweeping modern-ization of Russia's conventional arsenals… Russia has been particularly concerned about the so-called Prompt Global Strike program under development in the US, which would be capable of striking targets anywhere in the world in as little as an hour with deadly precision. The new doctrine mentioned the US program as a major destabilizing factor along with NATO missile defense plans.

Well, that is the gist of Russia's new Military Doctrine as reported by the Associated Press. In the 1960s, this Russian doctrine would have created a world-wide fear of nuclear war. Today, people believe that world leaders have more sense than to start such a war.

Nevertheless, former Soviet leader Mikhail Gorbachev is taking Russia's new Military Doctrine more seriously, and warning the world that the crisis in Ukraine could lead to a major war, even a nuclear war. Gorbachev accused the West and NATO of destroying the structure of European security by expanding its alliance. "No head of the Kremlin can ignore such a thing," he said, adding that the US was unfortunately starting to establish a "mega empire."

My concern is more basic: Vladimir Putin is an educated man, and he has enough smarts to retain the leadership of a superpower for many years. Why would he agree to sign such a doctrine? What are his political motivations behind this document? Does he really think the US and NATO will be scared by it? Or is his underlying intent to impress smaller nations?

I have a great respect for Mr. Putin's intellect, and these questions bother me. In my observation, powerful leaders usually have an ulterior motive behind what may look like a senseless move to ordinary people. Perhaps the answer is simply this: Perhaps Mr. Putin just wants to assure the Russian people that Russia will not be pushed around or threatened by NATO or the US.

I can fully understand why nations may wish to arm themselves with nuclear weapons as a deterrent to other nations' threat of war, but I do not believe any of these nations will ever use nuclear weapons, even as a last resort, because it would mean their own destruction. That is why I think the nuclear-weapon threat is no more than a nuclear-weapon tease.

Early Philosophies

Philosophical speculations and opinions go all the way back to prehistoric times, when parents passed on their superstitions and wisdom to their children, when clan leaders showed their followers how to survive and how to kill their enemies, and when witch doctors taught tribal members ways to appease their gods; but, unfortunately, none of their accumulated, collective wisdom reached us in a written record.

Philosophy is based on speculations and opinions, of course; if it were based on facts, it would be a science. Recorded philosophical speculations and opinions only go back to the sixth century BC, both in Europe and in Asia. Ancient Greek philosophers developed new approaches to explain things, breaking away from mythology. Outstanding is Thales of Miletus, who is the reputed father of Greek philosophy. He proclaimed water to be the basis of all things. In this regard, he would probably get no argument from scientists, especially those who look for water on other planets to sustain life. Heraclitus of Ephesus assumed that all things originate from fire. He probably had the Sun in mind, which also makes sense. Pythagoras of Samos coined the word philosophy, i.e., in the Greek language: the love of wisdom. He aspired to persuade human beings to lead a harmonious life. Xenophanes of Colophon was the father of pantheism. For him, God was the eternal unity pervading the universe, governing it by thought. Parmenides of Elea insisted that being alone is true, rather than being in a changing multitude, which he considered an appearance without reality. His younger countryman Zeno agreed with him and set out a number of paradoxes to show that believing in change or multiplicity only leads to contradictions. Zeno's legacy is that philosophers who followed him became aware of the difficulty of handling the concept of infinity. Anaxagoras of Clazomenae conceived divine reason to provide order in the world. He also first established philosophy in Athens. Leucippus and his pupil Democritus of Abdera first established an explicitly materialistic system, essentially the doctrine of atoms.

Following these earlier philosophers was Socrates of Athens. He questioned people relentlessly about their beliefs. He also disbelieved in the gods of Athens, and was eventually executed for this belief and for corrupting the youths of Athens with his beliefs. His method of questioning, however, did not establish certainties about any virtues; it just exposed the ignorance of his fellow debaters. Antisthenes of Athens, the founder of the Cynics, believed that the highest good is the virtue that rejects every enjoyment. On the other hand, Aristippus of Cyrene, the founder of Cyrenaics, regarded virtue as good only if it contributed to pleasure. Plato of Athens developed a unity of understanding using previous philosophical speculations. He also divided philosophy into dialectic, ethics, and physics. Plato also founded a school called Academy. Aristotle of Stagira was an esteemed pupil of Plato – both shared the title of the greatest philosopher of antiquity. However, Aristotle liked to start from fact given by experience – philosophy meant science. He believed that living beings have a moving principle: the soul. In plants, the soul consists of nutrition; in animals, it consists of nutrition and sensation; and in humans it consists of nutrition, sensation, and intellectual activity; its perfect form would be reason separated from the body, thus being imperishable.

The followers of Aristotle, the Peripatetics, almost abandoned metaphysical speculations, some in favor of natural science, others in favor of more popular treatment of ethics. They also aimed to make philosophy the exclusive possession of the educated, depriving the masses of its benefit.

In India, similar philosophical speculations

developed starting with the sixth century BC. Siddhartha Gautama, commonly known as the Buddha, actively developed Buddhism, a non-theistic religion. He was recognized by his followers as the "awakened" or "enlightened" teacher. Buddhism's purpose is to avoid suffering, and its ultimate aim is the attainment of the sublime state of nirvana, i.e., the release from karma, or the sum of a person's actions in previous states of existence, since reincarnation takes place until enlightenment is attained. Buddhism spread throughout Asia, all the way to Japan. Another religion that took hold in India at that time is Jainism, founded by Rishabha. It prescribes nonviolence towards all living beings. The universe is eternal, and many gods exist. Reincarnation takes place until liberation.

In China, at about the same time, Confucius founded Confucianism. It teaches that the purpose of life is to fulfill one's role in society with respectability, honor, and loyalty. China also started other major schools, like Legalism, Taoism, Mohism, Naturalism, and Agrarianism.

One popular speculation is that Jesus Christ, in his "lost years" of possible travel, probably attained much of his own philosophy from various Asian religions, which also affects the Christian religion.

Human Strengths & Weaknesses

One, and probably the most important, strength of human beings is the ability to reason: If "A" equals "B" and "B" equals "C" than "C" must equal "A" – other animals do not possess this ability to reason. Unfortunately, human beings do not always make use of this strength, and this neglect is one of their weaknesses. Furthermore, logical thinking does not always lead to logical actions.

Since most other human strengths are similar to those of other animals, let's concentrate on some human weaknesses.

For some reason, human beings seem more prone to catch diseases. This may be due to unhealthier living practices – consumption of nicotine, alcohol, sugar, and so on. Human beings also seem to have a worse physical and mental decline with age than other animals.

Human beings submit more to their vanities than other animals do; this weakness causes them all kinds of problems; for example, a recent study showed that vanity, especially narcissism, is on the rise with men, causing stress-related illnesses, such as high blood pressure. I covered vanity extensively in my book *Oddities*. The following is an excerpt:

"Vanity of vanities," said the Preacher, "vanity of vanities; all is vanity."[*] Later, he added, "I have seen all the works that are done under the sun; and, behold, all *is* vanity and vexation of the spirit."[†]

If all is vanity, as the Preacher claimed, then we must closely examine not only worthless but also what we may consider "worthwhile" human endeavors. For example, when we offer our services to other people, are we doing so altruistically, for financial gain, or merely to feed our vanities? If we answer this question honestly, we may surprise ourselves. However, if the Preacher meant that the ultimate vanity exceeds all other vanities, then, indeed, we must add his comment to our list of oddities, but we must also ask ourselves the question, what is the ultimate vanity?

Human beings also like to hoard material goods, which is rare in the animal world. In most cases these material goods, other than clothing and housing, serve little practical purpose and are eventually discarded. Some of this trait has its root in greed. Greed is certainly one of the worst of human weaknesses. It often leads to wanting one's cake and eating it too.

Warring seems to be a strangely adored human tendency. This may be why some human beings do not

---

[*] Ecclesiastes 1:2
[†] Ecclesiastes 1:14

mind following leaders who have a strong desire to go to war – a despicable human trait. Perhaps this is also the reason why human beings have an almost insurmountable difficulty loving their enemies. The easier human behavior is to hate their enemies, and to seek revenge for even the smallest wrongdoing they experience by their fellow human beings.

Furthermore, it seems easier to blame others for wrongdoings than looking at one's own wrongdoing. Jealousies and envy are additional human weaknesses that can easily lead to hatred and to war.

Human beings are often guided by beliefs that are not scientifically supported. Gullibility is certainly a detrimental human weakness. This is why con artists are so successful. Con artists are experts at deceit, another human trait that can be called a weakness. Deceit is not only practiced by con artists but also by others, such as spouses who seek extramarital relationships, or people who are traitors.

Another human weakness is when human beings scorn their differences. Whites think they are superior to blacks; Gentiles think they are superior to Jews, and vice versa; one nation's people think they are superior to another nation's people; lawyers and doctors think they are superior to ordinary laborers; et cetera, et cetera. These beliefs are rooted in an overdeveloped egocentricity – a very disgraceful human trait.

On balance, I think human weaknesses outweigh human strengths, although the human reasoning strength also leads to remarkable human progress. It is too bad that this remarkable human progress is often misdirected, which is the ultimate human weakness. The following chapters highlight some human weaknesses.

Aspiration to be President

Quite a number of American citizens have the aspiration to become the president of the United States of America, but very few have the qualifications for the job, and even if they had the qualifications, they must also appeal to and be liked by the American people who elect them. First, of course, they must seek the nomination of one of the major parties, unless they wish to run as an independent. Then, the parties will weigh their qualifications and their appeal to evaluate the chances of being elected, and then nominate their choices. After party nomination, the candidates' campaign works to win the approval and majority of the people to get elected.

A candidate for president must be near perfect to win an election. He or she must have the charisma of a president; his or her background, religion, and education must be acceptable to the people; furthermore, his or her position on the election issues must not only be approved by the party that nominated him or her, but, more importantly, must be approved by the majority of the people at large, and that is quite a trick, because on many issues the position of the people may be evenly split – for and against.

There are at least three dozen election issues that a candidate must address and advance his or her position on: the country's economy, especially if unemployment is rampant; the war on terrorism, which is foremost on everyone's mind; crime and gun control; national healthcare as well as seniors' care and pensions; education; environmental risks, possible water shortage, and evident climate change; illegal immigrants; foreign policy and foreign relations; the country's lasting energy supply; the use of "dirty" oil; America's claim to arctic resources; free-trade agreements; subsidies and desirable trade protection; human rights and privacy issues; equality and racial issues; police brutality; abortion versus pro-life; gay marriages; corruption issues; the candidate's personal values; and so on. By the time the candidate has addressed all of these election issues, often during debates with other candidates, the people will have had a good chance to assess his or her character and potential leadership abilities.

Presently (early 2015) two excellent candidates for the American presidency have come forward: Hillary Diane Rodham Clinton, born October 26th 1947, and John Ellis "Jeb" Bush, born February 11th 1953. I have already expressed my admiration for Hillary Clinton in my book *Conclusions Volume II* (see page 53). Hillary has impressive experiences: as First Lady during Bill Clinton's presidency 1993-2001, as US Senator for New York 2001-2009, and as Secretary of State for President Barack Obama. Furthermore, she was a leading candidate for the US presidency during the 2008 election campaign. Very impressive!

Jeb Bush is also a very personable and likable chap with leadership ability. The American people may vote him in simply because he will come across like a breath of fresh air. Hillary, on the other hand, even with her impressive experience, may come across as too arrogant. She may borrow too many election slogans from her husband's campaign in 1992, and the American people might resent it. So, if the American people are willing to set aside experience, I have the feeling they may prefer Jeb Bush over Hillary Clinton, unless a more qualified candidate emerges during the impending election campaign.

Aspiring presidents must not unduly criticize their opponents. In an interview with NPR's Steve Inskeek on December 29th 2014, US President Barack Obama criticized his political opponents who claimed he had been outdone by Russia's president:

"You'll recall that three or four months ago, everybody in Washington was convinced that

President Putin was a genius and he had outmaneuvered all of us and he had bullied and strategized his way into expanding Russian power," he said. "Today, I'd sense that at least outside of Russia, maybe some people are thinking what Putin did wasn't so smart." Mr. Obama argued that sanctions had made the Russian economy vulnerable to "inevitable" disruptions in oil prices, which, when they came, led to "enormous difficulties." "The big advantage we have with Russia is we've got a dynamic, vital economy, and they don't," he said. "They rely on oil. We rely on oil and iPads and movies and you name it."

However, President Vladimir Putin is still popular in Russia; he certainly has more popular staying power than his US counterparts. Former Russian President Boris Yeltsin chose his Prime Minster, Vladimir Putin, to succeed him after he retired December 31st 1999, and Vladimir Putin is still Russia's president in 2015.

Not all US presidents get elected for a second term. Even when they get elected for a second term, some presidents lose their original popularity. For aspiring presidents, it is not only important to be popular at election time, but to stay popular during their term in office.

Follow the Leader

People's desire to follow a leader is prevalent. All throughout history and probably as far back as human existence, people followed a leader, or a group of leaders, albeit often to their detriment. Not that all leaders who led their followers to devastation had this result of their leadership in mind, but their actions made this outcome inevitable. Quite often, when leaders acquire power it can corrupt them and their minds, and very few leaders can resist this trend. Nero, Napoleon, Kaiser William II, Paul von Hindenburg, Hitler, Stalin, Mussolini, to name a few, all went that way.

Nevertheless, it is easier for people to follow a leader than to lead, especially when critical issues become involved. For example, Adolf Hitler surfaced when the German people faced several critical issues: The Treaty of Versailles; hyperinflation; severe unemployment; widespread depression; and so on. Hitler merely had to promise the German people salvation from these tribulations, using his oratory skills, and his leadership election was assured. Nobody foresaw the evils that followed his election.

On a smaller scale, leaders of religious groups can also cause devastation for their followers. For example, on November 18th 1978, the religious leader Jim Jones led 909 American members of the Peoples Temple to commit suicide in Jonestown, Guyana. They were convinced to commit "an act of revolutionary suicide protesting the conditions of an inhumane world." From 1994 to 1997 Joseph Di Mambro led circa 74 members of the Order of the Solar Temple to commit suicide. Mambro convinced them that their deaths would be an escape from the hypocrisies and oppression of this world, and that they were moving to Sirius. On March 26th 1997, Marshall Herff Applewhite, the leader of the cult Heaven's Gate, led 39 followers to commit mass suicide in Rancho Santa Fe, California. They believed they were exiting their human vessels for their souls to go on a journey aboard a spaceship, following the comet Hale-Bopp.

One of the strangest religious leaderships came from Credonia Mwerinde. She was part of a triumvirate, including Joseph Kibweteere and Dominic Kataribaabo, that led a break-away sect of the Roman Catholic Church in Uganda, called the Movement of the Restoration of the Ten Commandments of God, which was founded in 1989. Mwerinde predicted an apocalypse after the end of 1999, and, as the new millennium approached, sect members sold their properties and turned the profits over to the leadership. However, when the world did not end on January 1st 2000, the sect members asked questions and demanded the return of their money. Mwerinde quickly initiated a purge of the membership, culminating in the destruction of its Kanangu Church in a fire that killed 530 members. Other killings else-where in Uganda brought the final death total of the membership to 778. The police's first assumption of mass suicide was later investigated as mass murder. Furthermore, the police believed that Credonia Mwerinde and Joseph Kibweteere survived the killings and issued an international arrest warrant for them in this connection. Nevertheless, the why, how, what, where, and when still remain mysteries to this day. Eleven years later, in 2011, Credonia Mwerinde, along with four other prophesiers, was awarded the Ig Nobel Prize for "teaching the world to be careful when making mathematical assumptions and calculations."

Although these devastations caused by religious leaders are very sad and despicable, the devastations of world leaders caused during WWI and WWII are far worse and more despicable. During WWI, nearly 18 million people were killed and an additional 23.6 million wounded. This was topped during WWII, when an estimated 85 million people were killed and an additional 22.5 million wounded. The deaths of civilians jumped from 4.8 million during WWI to an estimated 55 million during WWII – a despicable insanity hard to comprehend, but this was the result of following our esteemed leaders.

Of course, had it not been for enforced drafts, many people would have refused to join the armed forces that caused such incomprehensible destruction and devastation.

Greed, Envy & Corruption

Greed often amasses huge hoards, even if not needed. Compared to greedy billionaires, millionaires today are almost paupers. A total of 1,645 people in the world made the 2014 billionaire list. Their combined wealth came to US $6.4 trillion, an average of US $3.89 billion per billionaire. Without a doubt, none of these billionaires would even need one-thousandth of his or her wealth accumulation to lead an exceptionally comfortable life. Such personal greed is at the extreme, of course, but it serves as a demonstration of what greed can accomplish.

On the national side, we have the greed of leaders who wish to expand the territory of their countries. In the 1930s, German Chancellor Adolf Hitler convinced himself, and tried to convince the German people, that the German people needed more *Lebensraum* – living space. In fact, this was not true in the 1930s, and it is not true today. Today, nobody in the German government even thinks about such nonsense. A more recent greedy acquisition occurred when the Russian President Vladimir Putin approved Russia's annexation of the Ukrainian Crimea Peninsula, which caused uproar in the western world.

Greed is closely tied to envy. Many people do not need anything better or bigger, but their envy of friends or neighbors convinces them that they must have it, too. One wonders to what extent envy exists among world leaders. X has more armories, so Y must have them too, and Z follows suit. This occurred when the USSR envied the USA its atom bomb in 1945, and a few smaller countries followed suit. There is a widespread envy between various nations in the world. There is also widespread envy between competing companies, but such envy often benefits the consumer.

A very serious form of greed usually leads to corruption, mainly political corruption. Here is some interesting information from the Wikipedia regarding political corruption:

> Political corruption is the use of power by government officials for illegitimate private gain. S. D. Morris, professor of politics, wrote in his book *Corruption & Politics in Contemporary Mexico* (University of Alabama Press, Tuscaloosa, 1991) that "corruption is the illegitimate use of public power to benefit a private interest." The economist Dr. Daniel Kaufmann extends the concept to include 'legal corruption' in which power is abused within the confines of the law –

as those with power often have the ability to shape the law for their protection.* A state of unrestrained political corruption is known as a kleptocracy, literally meaning "rule of thieves." This type of government is generally considered corrupt, and the mechanism of action is often embezzlement of state funds. Forms of corruption vary, but include bribery, extortion, cronyism, nepotism, patronage, graft, and embezzlement. Worldwide, bribery alone is estimated to involve over one trillion US dollars annually.

We have also "institutional corruption," which arises in an institution that depends on financial support from people who have private interests that may conflict with the primary purpose of the institution (Wikipedia). For example, parents who bestow financial support to a college may put pressure on the college to certify their unworthy offspring.

So, is envy or jealousy an ungodly trait? The answer is "no," at least as far as the Biblical God is concerned: "Thou shalt not make unto thee any graven image, or any likeness of anything that is in heaven

---

* Dr. Daniel Kaufmann is the president of the Natural Resource Governance Institute, formerly the Revenue Watch Institute - Natural Resource Charter. Previously he was a senior fellow at the Brookings Institution. Prior to that, he was a director at the World Bank Institute, leading work on governance and anti-corruption.

above, or that is in the earth beneath, or that is in the water under the earth: thou shalt not bow down thyself to them, nor serve them: for I the Lord thy God am a jealous God, visiting the iniquity of the fathers upon the children unto the third and fourth generation of them that hate me; and shewing mercy unto thousands of them that love me, and keep my commandments."[*]
Even Paul the Apostle warned the Corinthians not to provoke God's jealousy: "Do we provoke the Lord to jealousy? Are we stronger than he?"[†]

There can be no doubt that greed, envy, and corruption are abominable human traits. Even if they appear to be godly, they create nothing but harm.

---

[*] Exodus 20:4-6
[†] 1 Corinthians 10:22

Rude & Mean

When World War Two ended in Germany, I had just turned eleven. Six years later, I landed in Canada to join my maternal grandparents. In 1930, my grandfather had decided that Canada was the land of opportunity for him and promptly sailed off yonder to the land where milk and honey flows.

At first, I was unimpressed with the land where milk and honey flows. I met up with crude conditions and some cruel attitudes toward Germans, and I would have appreciated a return ticket to Germany. I even had to start a new apprenticeship as an electrician, because I failed to find employment to make use of my German apprenticeship as a precision instrument mechanic. Nevertheless, after the end of my second apprenticeship, I had fallen in love with Canada, and I applied for its citizenship, which I never regretted.

In 1973, I paid a visit to Germany, the land of my birth, and encountered a few disappointments. I met too many narrow-minded, selfish, and rude people, and some of them were outright mean. I was glad to return to open-minded Canada. A year earlier, Bill Bryson experienced similar unfriendly treatments in

Paris, France.[*] I should also mention the mean treatment our family received from the German Post Office when we wanted to cash in our lives' savings. My parents had established a bank account for each of us children and one for my mother. After WWII, the German Post Office took charge of the bank's assets, and we applied to the Post Office to release our savings. The Post Office acknowledged that the money was available for our accounts, but refused to release it without the receipt of our bank books, which, of course, were lost to the bombings during the war. Due to this refusal, we children only lost a few hundred marks each, but my mother lost a few thousand marks. I can only say, "Thanks Germany for being so inconsiderate to needy families who lost everything during a war they never wanted! I hope you make good use of our confiscated bank accounts!"

Recently, I read Leni Riefenstahl's book *A Memoir*, and I was appalled by the way the Germans and the French treated her after the war (WWII). Although one could expect this from the vanquished French, Leni Riefenstahl did not expect it. When the Americans vacated a part of their occupation zone to let the French occupy it, they advised Leni to leave with them; they even offered to move her belongings for her; but Leni decided to stay, because she thought

---

[*] See his book *Neither Here Nor There – Travels in Europe* page 41.

she had developed a good relationship with the French – a decision she soon regretted, after the French confiscated her property and treated her like a criminal.

However, the mean treatments she later received from the Germans, her own countrymen, could not have been anticipated by her, especially since she was held in high regard worldwide. Her treatment by the German people only confirmed my own experience, especially Germany's mean confiscation of our bank accounts.

In Leni Riefenstahl's film *Triumph of the Will*, it was evident to me that Hitler's speeches tried to uplift the spirit and national pride of the German people. His speeches were devoid of racism, and he may have accomplished his goal. However, what he may not have expected is that his racism, mostly expressed in his book *My Struggle*, awoke a natural meanness in some of the German people, which eventually led to the atrocities of the concentration camps. I doubt if Hitler even realized the full extent of the meanness his racial attitude had invoked in some German people. Yes, he hated the Jews, but did he hate them enough to expunge them? Hitler also admired some Jews, such as his family's doctor, and he tried to ship Jews to other countries. Perhaps by expressing his hatred of the Jews, he merely incited the meanest instincts of some mean Germans to carry out what they believed he meant them to do.

Whenever we encounter rude, mean people it is probably best to follow Pearl S. Buck's advice and turn our backs to them – and run away if possible. This is, no doubt, what saved the lives of those people (and not all of them Jews) that turned their backs on Germany during Hitler's reign.

Torture & Abuse

Torture of human beings (and animals) probably goes all the way back to prehistoric times. Although torture has been banned by many countries throughout the world, it is still being practiced extensively, especially during interrogations, and along with torture comes physical and psychological abuse. However, it is surprising to what extent the US Central Intelligence Agency (CIA) practiced interrogation torture after the 9/11 terrorists' attack. This CIA practice was published in a report by Democrats on the intelligence committee on December 9th 2014, and Andy Sully of BBC News reported the following on December 10th 2014:

> The report - by Democrats on the intelligence committee - accuses the agency of using brutal "enhanced interrogation techniques", lying to the White House, and exaggerating its successes. The CIA – which fought to have the report suppressed – says its conclusions are flawed. The Independent calls the publication a cue for "America's day of shame". Its subheading says:

"Report shows the CIA tortured suspects at secret overseas sites for years, achieved nothing from it, and lied about it". The paper says the report's details of the interrogation of an unknown number of al-Qaeda suspects in the wake of the September 11 attacks are "so replete with details of barbarism and inhumane treatment as to call into question the values at the core of the nation's identity." The paper lists the treatment meted out to detainees at "black site" secret prisons around the world, including being kept awake for up to 180 hours; being shackled and held in stress positions for days; being waterboarded repeatedly in "a series of near drownings"; having their families threatened, and being force-fed via the rectum. Some were also subjected to extremes of cold and heat, and it is accepted by the agency that one man died of hypothermia at an Afghan secret prison. The Independent adds that the senate committee found these techniques were "not effective" ways to gather intelligence... The Times notes that the UN has said America has a "legal duty" to prosecute those responsible for torture, and Amnesty International has called for the perpetrators to be "held accountable". The Times also lists ways in which the interrogations yielded mainly useless information. The paper says Khalid Sheikh Mohammed, the supposed instigator of the 9/11 plot, was waterboarded 183 times because he did not reveal the details of a plot which was later discovered never to have existed. During the simulated drownings, the jihadist fabricated a plot to recruit black Muslims in the Midwest, in an effort to get his captors to stop the torture. The Daily Telegraph says the report also throws light into the way the CIA lied about its operations, "exaggerating the importance of information obtained under torture to justify its actions" and falsely claiming to have "cracked a plot" to crash hijacked planes into Heathrow Airport. The paper says even the US president was "hoodwinked" by misleading briefings from the CIA. The Guardian reports a company formed by two psychologists to develop the "enhanced techniques" received $81m from the agency between 2002 and 2009, when its contract was terminated. It quotes Mark Fallon, a US Navy investigator who interrogated detainees but did not use torture techniques. He tells the paper the CIA's program was "illegal, ineffective, immoral and inconsistent with American values. Al-Qaeda used what we did to recruit more terrorists, so we have to ask how much damage torture did to our national security, not how much damage the report has done." In its comment page, the Daily Mail says the revelations were "a truly black day for the 'civilized' West. This devastating report finds the CIA systematically violated every precept and value that we believe makes us better than our enemies, from the rule of law and observance of treaty obligations to the dictates of common humanity."... It notes: "As for Britain, it is impossible to tell how deeply the Blair Government was implicated in the CIA's program. For any references to MI5, MI6 or Diego Garcia, the British territory used for rendition flights, have been redacted from the report, presumably under diplomatic pressure from Downing Street."... [And] The Times leader column comments, "The world's remaining tyrants will read this report carefully. Its best lesson is that when America loses its way it works hard to recover the moral high ground."... The Daily Telegraph features a commentary from former CIA director Michael Hayden. Mr. Hayden says the report's authors did not talk to anyone involved in the CIA's program, but if they did "they would have had to deal with our absolute assurance that this program led to the capture of senior Al-Qaeda operatives (including helping to find Osama bin Laden)...

and led to the disruption of terrorist plots, saving American and Allied lives. The Senate Democrat document reads like a shrill prosecutorial screed rather than a dispassionate historical study. What happened here seems clear: The staff started with a conclusion and then 'cherry picked' their way through 6 million pages of documents, ignoring some data and highlighting others, to make their case."

Michael Hayden may well be correct, but does this justify inhumane treatment of suspects by interrogators? Nevertheless, the question is moot, because the interrogators will unlikely be held accountable for their actions. Here again, we have a situation where "might" is right.

Another type of abuse is fatigue and burnout. Every one of us can experience fatigue; even entire nations can experience fatigue; materials can develop fatigue as well, which is important to avoid in aircraft design. When fatigue occurs in people, or entire nations, measures are required for their revitalization, because sometimes fatigue can lead to burnout. However, burnout can also occur without fatigue – for example, through loss of interest.

People experience loss-of-interest burnout surprisingly often. One frequently hears the comment:

"I'm sick and tired of...this or that." It could be a straining job or relationship; it could be an unwanted habit; it could be a fading fad; it could be an obnoxious object or a pet or a person; it could be almost anything that bothers people and eventually causes them to lose interest and develop a feeling of burnout. In other words, they become sick and tired of it or him or her or them.

Businesses should become aware when people, by and large, experience burnout with their products. This is the time to offer them a new product to retain their interest. The same applies to politicians or to other public servants. They may be doing their jobs perfectly well, but, at some point, people have had enough of them and want a change.

A nation's burnout can occur when its people went through a trying time, like a war or a depression. At this time, understanding and creative leaders are required to revitalize the nation. [This happened in the USA during the 1930s and in Germany after WWII.]

Wars and terrorism may prevail, but we must surely try to eliminate torture and abuse of our fellow human beings.

Fatalism, Eternity & Sin

The Peerage Reference Dictionary defines a fatalist as "a person who accepts and submits to what happens, regarding it as inevitable." Fatalism is also connected with determinism, which is defined as "a doctrine that human action is not free but determined by motives regarded as external force acting on the will" and with predestination, which is defined as "the doctrine that God has foreordained all that happens, or that certain souls are destined for salvation and eternal life and others are not."

The fatalist's stance is one of complete submission to a supremacy that controls the world. In other words, God made it happen that way, and nothing we do can change it, because whatever we do is also what God wanted us to do to achieve His desired outcome. The same applies to nature, and that is the true fatalism.

Fatalistic attitudes are not uncommon in the world. I heard a vicar tell a woman who had just lost her daughter, "These things are sent to try us." In other words, God allowed her daughter to die to test her reaction to the loss, her belief in God, and His wisdom. This may not sound fatalistic, but it is when you think about it. My maternal grandmother told me one time, "Everything is designed that way." She religiously believed that all things that happen follow God's design. Furthermore, we often hear people say, "God willing, we shall meet next week in good health." Again, this does not sound fatalistic, but it is if people believe that God can prevent their meeting in good health.

A farmer walks through his field during a thunderstorm and is struck dead by a lightning bolt. A fatalist tells you it was God's will that prevailed. A scientist tells you that the occurrence was natural, since the farmer was the only elevated conductor to ground in the field. The problem is that the scientist's explanation will not change the mind of the fatalist, who believes that God makes use of natural phenomena to serve His purposes. A fatalist may point out that lightning does not always strike a person in an open field, therefore, when it happens, it must have happened because God willed it to happen and not because it was an automatic, natural occurrence.

Fatalism likes God, whose own creation is unknown and probably unknowable, and God creates all else and all that happens in the universe. Most fatalists believe that all that comes to pass happens with God's knowledge and approval – a pretty simple belief when it comes right down to it, since all other explanations are more complex.

I am a firm believer in cause and effect; however, this belief can also present some problems, and could even be a type of fatalism, since both the cause and the effect may be inevitable. Heat applied to water causing steam to form is one example of cause and effect, but the cause of this event can be quite complex, although the effect appears straightforward. With every cause-and-effect principle, one can rightfully ask, "and what causes the cause?" In the case of applying heat to water to get steam, the reply could be, "heat is caused by burning oil or gas, or by the sun, or by electricity," but this answer only gives you the cause of the cause one step back; going further back may prove to be quite involved. In fact, we may never find an answer all the way back to the beginning – providing there ever was a beginning, which I doubt.

Scientists who believe that the universe will eventually revert back to its microscopic point that caused the Big Bang are also fatalists when you think about it. Any person who believes in inescapable future events could be called a fatalist, because he or she believes that these future events are preordained, whether by God or by nature.

One belief is that all that happens in the universe and the world is subject to inevitable universal laws.

Nothing that happens can happen against these universal laws. One can try to break these laws, but that does not eliminate them. People who think they can break these universal laws are only kidding themselves, because these laws remain and will eventually prevail. This belief, too, is a form of fatalism. In fact, some people believe that these universal laws are truly God, instead of God being some human-like individual, although omnipotent.

The point is, don't scorn fatalists until you have examined their and your own beliefs; the outcome may surprise you.

Another questionable belief is the belief in eternal life. I was sitting at a table in a shopping plaza's food court one day, trying to relax for a few minutes, when a young Negro put a tract published by the Deeper Christian Life Ministry in front of me. Normally, I ignore such tracts, but this one caught my attention because of its title: Eternity. In its first paragraph, the tract stated, "Eternity has no end." Then, in its second paragraph, it continued as follows:

> Suppose it were possible to tie a rope from earth to heaven and an ant were to go to the sun and return to earth on this rope. When an ant has done that a hundred times, then a small fraction of eternity has passed.

Ignoring all other nonsense in this statement, I draw your attention to "a small fraction of eternity." Note that a small fraction of anything implies a finite whole, regardless of the size of the fraction. The tract also tells us that we can spend eternity either with God or with Satan. However, it goes on to say that "Life without God is a hopeless *end*." (Emphasis mine) In other words, eternity with Satan does have an end to it, and, therefore, cannot be endless. Not that this verbiage surprises me. Even educated people have problems with the concept of eternity. Nevertheless, the publishers of such tracts should be more careful in their use of abstract concepts.

In this tract, eternal life with God is only the carrot, of course, to get you to repent your sins, so that you do not have to spend eternal life in hell with Satan, which is the stick.

Ah, yes, sins: the Deeper Christian Life Ministry wisely avoided in its tract to explain what it meant by sins – I suspect so as not to turn off its readers. Mormons consider it a sin to drink tea or coffee; Muslims consider it a sin to drink wine, beer, or other alcoholic spirits; devout Jews consider it a sin to eat pork; Hindus consider it a sin to eat beef; most countries consider it a sin to kill people, except when you do it for your country. I asked my only living uncle recently why he turned from being a Baptist to being a Pentecostal, and he said to me, "Because Baptists use water." He was so sincere that I held my tongue telling him that even Jesus Christ allowed John the Baptist to use water when he baptized him.

There are probably as many variations of sin as there are variations of religions and religious sects. If you are addicted to a sin, you can probably find a religion or a sect to support your addiction. I had a boss one time who kept a mistress besides his loving wife; he eventually joined the Mormons to get support for his sin. Catholics go to confession to get support and rid themselves of their sins. Thus, one way or another, we can find assurances somewhere that our so-called sins will not prevent us from joining God for eternity. Good Luck in your search for such assurances!

As a time concept, eternity is a more likely event than a beginning and an end. Through conditioning, human beings probably prefer a beginning and an end; for example, the sperm enters the ovum; that's the beginning of a human being, and death is the end. Vanity, another human trait, assumes that the human soul is so important that it must have, or be given, the ability to live forever, and this vanity and the fear of death is what religion leaders count on to try and sell eternal life or reincarnation to prospective believers.

The Duality Principle

Our entire world is made up of dualities: east/west, north/south, black/white, up/down, male/female, and so on. It takes two to tango, as the saying goes.

In the chapter *Questionable Odds & Ends* of my book *Thoughts in a Maze*, I posed the question: Which came first, the chicken or the egg? I challenged our scientists to provide us with the answer. My readers may have assumed that I was joking, but I was dead serious. Plants scatter their seeds to create new plants, but we have to start with one plant to create the seeds of other plants. We know that a chicken lays eggs and sits on them for a while to brood new chickens, but nobody ever told us where the first chicken came from to lay these eggs.

The same applies to human beings. Darwin takes human beings back to apes, but human beings go much further back. The human male has a sperm that enters the ovum of the human female and, thus, a new human being is born, but where did the first human male sperm and the first human female ovum come from to create human beings? Our religious folks may point to the Bible for the answer, but our scientists still consider this question puzzling.

The duality principle simply says that we cannot create one part of duality without creating the other part, and we cannot destroy one part of duality without destroying the other part. This principle cannot be ignored no matter how hard we try. Many religions claim the existence of a good and a bad cosmic spirit; hence, to know what's good we need bad to compare; furthermore, old can only exist if we also have young, and so on.

Some of my readers may remember the appendix *Why I Am a Christian* in my book *Connections*. In it, I relate Bertrand Russell's criticism of Christ for believing in hell, which Russell thought was no longer required of a Christian because of a judgment of the Lords of the Judicial Committee of the British Privy Council on the Appeal of Jenkins v. Cook, from the Arches Court of Canterbury (February 16th 1876).

Henry Jenkins had put together a book of Bible excerpts that omitted all passages to the devil and evil spirits, and Flavel Cook, the vicar of his parish, refused to administer the Sacrament of the Holy Communion to Mr. Jenkins because of his omissions. A few letters went back and forth between Mr. Jenkins and Mr. Cook, which were also submitted in evidence. After an exhaustive examination of the Statute 1 of Edward VI, chap. 1, sect. 8, plus the Rubric and the

Canons, their Lordships came to the conclusion, and judgment, that none of these documents, or Mr. Jenkins's behavior, supported causes to deny him the Sacrament of the Holy Communion. From this judgment, the assumption arose that Christians, to their utter relief, were no longer required to believe in hell.

I mention the Jenkins-versus-Cook case again here because of its apparent abandonment of the duality principle. Regardless whether hell exists or not, hell is needed by the duality principle to offset heaven, even though heaven may also be nonexistent. I think Mr. Cook should have merely pointed out to Mr. Jenkins that hell simply offsets heaven, and, therefore, should not be omitted from his book of Bible excerpts. I also think that Bertrand Russell, the renowned and respected twentieth-century philosopher, conveniently overlooked the duality principle when he delivered his disparaging comments on Christ's belief in hell.

Storm is differentiated from calm; rain from sunshine; heat from cold; good from evil; heaven from hell; God from Satan; the list goes on and on. There may be instances where the duality principle does not prevail, but they are rare and difficult to find. For example, take a stone in a field: could it have an opposite? It is unlikely but possible. The opposite may be the soil it sits on.

The important point is that all of us need to become more aware of the duality principle in life, so that we do not develop the tendency of omitting, ignoring, or disbelieving in the necessity of one of its dual parts.

Design Flaws

Human designs are seldom without flaws: Buildings, bridges, and mines collapse; automobiles are recalled to correct flaws; ferry boats are capsizing; airplanes and even spaceships are crashing; computer programs must be debugged and eventually updated to add missing functions; military coups that could go wrong; food manufacturers producing toxic foods; the list is endless, but nature's designs also have flaws. At one time, we had a tree at the boulevard in front of our house, a very misshapen tree; we could hardly believe that nature could create anything uglier. So, are there any designs anywhere in the universe that are without flaws?

Our religious folks believe that God's designs must be without flaws, however, that, too, is questionable. Take the foreskin of a man's penis, for example. When God realized that this foreskin may prove to be more troublesome than it's worth, He issued a command to circumcise it,[*] and Jews have followed this command religiously, as a covenant with God. On the other hand, it seems that this covenant does not

---

[*] Genesis 17:10-14

apply to Christians.[*] In any case, remember that prior to making this covenant, God had created man in His own image.[†]

Still, if we believe that everything in nature is God's design, we cannot find too many flaws, and that is truly remarkable.[‡] Nevertheless, there are some death-threatening flaws that can only be restored to health by modern medical treatment. Take the appendix as an example: a vestigial organ with no known purpose that can get infected and cause death. In the USA, about 300,000 people have surgical treatment every year for appendicitis, and, worldwide, thousands of people die yearly from appendicitis. Take the pharynx as another example: a passage for ingestion as well as respiration, a design that often causes death by choking. In the USA alone, accidental deaths by choking come to 2,500 per year. As another example, take the childbirth canal, which passes through the female's pelvis, and if the baby's head is significantly larger than the pelvic opening, certain death of the mother and child at childbirth can only be surgically prevented. Those are just a few examples of poor design of the human body. In addition to design

---

[*] Paul told the Galatians, "Behold, I Paul say unto you, that if ye be circumcised, Christ shall profit you nothing." (Galatians 5:2)

[†] Genesis 1:27

[‡] Note that believers in God use this remarkable feat as proof of God's existence.

flaws in the human body, how many design flaws are there in our universe that can backfire?

One other noteworthy design flaw is the impossibility of "Peace on Earth." Some people send greeting cards, or display signs in their houses or on their lawns, with the message "Peace on Earth." The notion of "Peace on Earth" took hold after the Thirty Years' War.[*] The war involved almost all of Europe. People had spent their energies, spent their wealth, experienced health problems, and coped with eight million casualties; they were dispirited and outspokenly opposed to any more wars. Their earnest desire was to have peace on Earth forever, and they made sure to remind themselves of this message going forward.

Nevertheless, "Peace on Earth" is never going to happen, because people collectively will never be able to love their enemies, which they must do for "Peace on Earth" to take place. To believe otherwise, is to believe that the entire human race will eventually convert to Christianity. Not that Christians are more able to love their enemies than other religious groups, but because loving their enemies is one of the prerequisites to being a Christian.

However, even if some exceptional human beings are able to love their enemies, it is literally impossible

---

[*] From 1618 to 1648

for the entire human race or an entire nation to love its enemies! This may explain wars. The few people within a human race or a nation who could love their enemies are virtually vastly outnumbered and over-ruled by those who cannot or will not love their enemies and wish to go to war against them!

Furthermore, once a nation has been categorized as an enemy by other nations, it becomes difficult for that nation to escape this classification. Any and all actions by this nation will be viewed with suspicion by those nations who have earmarked it as an enemy, and that is a type of hatred as well.

People who naïvely believe that "Peace on Earth" can be achieved must disregard terrorists groups, and groups that create religion-sanctioned holy wars. They must also disregard human traits like hatred, and the urge for vengeance, envy, and greed, to name a few.

Those who like to send greeting cards with the message "Peace on Earth" should write instead: "Peace between Friends," at least that is within the realm of possibilities, although difficult enough to achieve, but not as impossible as "Peace on Earth."

When I use the word "never," I fully realize that "never" is a long time. Perhaps some miracle in the distant future will make "Peace on Earth" possible, but I do not believe it.

There is another enemy I would like to draw to

your attention. As I read John Simpson's book *Not Quite World's End*, I was looking for some special words of wisdom. Then I found them on the second-last page of his book:

> "On the kitchen wall of the house where we are staying [in South Africa] is a quotation from Carl Gustav Jung, Smuts' friend, which haunts me. There is a relevance to me and my life, I know, but I can't entirely grasp it. The meaning comes closer then moves away, like the yellow butter-flies in the patch of sunlight:
>
>> But what if I should discover that the very enemy himself is within me, that I myself am the enemy who must be loved – what then?"

When I read this quote by Carl Gustav Jung, it made me wonder if Jesus Christ had included the enemy within us when he gave us his command: "love thy enemy." If so, the difficulty of loving one's enemy takes on a new dimension. It may be easier for us to love an external enemy than the enemy within.

However, when loving an enemy within you must also support the enemy within. Is that even desirable? The enemy within may well be some disease that one wants to get rid of.

In any case, if you are one of those naïve souls who like to send the message "Peace on Earth" to friends, I hope that I have not entirely discouraged you. As a utopian goal, "Peace on Earth" is definitely desirable, but do not expect it to happen in the foreseeable future, if at all.

Appendix – The Group of Twenty-Two

At the end of a book, I usually pass on some notable or strange observation to my readers, and this book is no exception.

I had a strange dream recently. A small number of us took refuge in a hut from an angry mob that was trying to kill us. After locking the door, we sat around quietly, contemplating our fate, when a small man with a large, bald head – not shaven, just naturally bald – caught my attention. He had a serene expression, with a slight smile, and I asked him why he was not afraid. He said, "Because I belong to the group of twenty-two." Why twenty-two? I don't know. It was never explained to me, but there will always be twenty-two men and women in the world who have attained wisdom beyond the rest of us; if one of them gets killed, or dies of natural causes, another one will take his or her place.

After this dream, I was wondering: who in the world might have the wisdom to be part of this group of twenty-two? As you know, I try to follow the actions of our world leaders, and the one that came to mind was Angela Merkel. I would advise you to follow her actions for a while, and see if you will agree with me. Also, follow the actions of other world leaders, and try to determine who might fit the bill to be part of the group of twenty-two – not one who is famous, or powerful, but one who has attained wisdom beyond the rest of us.

About the Author

Arthur O.R. Thormann has many interests:
Poetry, writing, reading, teaching, consulting,
photography, trusteeships, philosophy,
and software development, to name a few.
Germany is his country of birth; Canada is his
country of choice; Edmonton, Alberta,
is his hometown.

www.ingramcontent.com/pod-product-compliance
Lightning Source LLC
Chambersburg PA
CBHW071829020426
42331CB00007B/1663